TEACHING CHRISTIANS

To Pray

THE BIBLE WAY

Revised and Expanded

I0201817

Nate Fortner

TEACHING CHRISTIANS

To Pray

THE BIBLE WAY

Revised and Expanded

Whosoever Press

What Others Are Saying About Nate Fortner and Teaching Christians to Pray the Bible Way...

Anyone, Christian or not, will be able to use this prayer journal as a tool to become closer to God, if that is his or her goal. Using example prayers, Scriptures, and even explanations of prayer principles, the author has created a structural device here that is not only practical but inspirational as well.

~Nate Fortner
Whosoever Press

"Teaching Christians to Pray the Bible Way" would be a great book for new Christians as well as those that have been Christians for years. It helps you realize that when we pray, it's just like talking to your earthly dad. No problem is too big or too small to pray about! It strengthens your faith by keeping a record of your prayers and how God answers them. It helps instill the importance of thanking God each time He answers your prayers!

~Debra Davidson
Lambert's Bible's and Gifts

I would highly recommend Nate Fortner's book "Teaching Christians to Pray the Bible Way." It will be good for all Christians but especially new babes in Jesus. It not only is bible based teaching it give the reader the chance to journal and explore for themselves the different kinds of prayer. I personally enjoyed the chapter on the Names of God. The ones I enjoy the most are Elohim, El Roi, El Shaddai, Jehovah and Jehovah-Jireh. Thank you Nate for a wonderful Christian work.

~*Pamela Owens-Sanderson RN*

Abundant Life Family Chiropractic

Teaching Christians To Pray the Bible Way encompasses all facets of prayer. Not only is this book important for a new believer in Christ, but it also is a breath of fresh air to the prayer life of seasoned Christians. You will find it very simple and easy to read, inspired by the Holy Spirit, and begin to see the prayers you pray being answered. Thank you, Nate, for your obedience to God's perfect will. And to all that read this book, may the hand of God be a mighty force in your life. Yours truly,

~ *Dr. Darla Lasseter RN, DC*

Abundant Life Family Chiropractic

Whosoever Press books may be ordered through booksellers or by contacting:

Whosoever Press
P.O. Box 1513
Boaz, Alabama 35957
www.NateFortnerMinistries.webs.com

www.WhosoeverPress.com
256-706-3315

ISBN-13: 978-0615831718 (sc)

Printed in the United States of America

Whosoever Press rev. date: 07/10/2013

To my family and friends. For my Grandpa Harold and best Childhood friend- John Luther. Also a special dedication to the Boaz Church of God. Since the first time I walked through the doors, I was warmly welcomed into the fold. When I was searching to belong, they accepted me for who I was. They didn't push up their noses and act like they were better than me. They didn't talk about me behind my back either. Of course, I found out later that they were talking good about me behind my back! Not only did I find a good church, but I found a home. Not only did I find a place to be, but a place to belong. Not only did I find a place to fit, but a place where I could fit in. When I found the Boaz Church of God, not only did I find a great church full of great Christian people, I found a family! Thank you church family! I love you all! Thank you Jesus!

When you ask God for something in prayer, sometimes He places someone or something in your life that will enable you to receive what you asked for!

~Nate Fortner

Contents

CHAPTER	PAGE
23 Principles Receiving Answered Prayers	16
911 Prayers	32
The Day I Prayed for Wisdom	34
Becoming A Joshua 24:15 Family	39
Learn To Pray Scripture	46
Intercessory Prayer	75
Coffee with Jesus	79
Praying the Names of God	82
Praying Songs	108
Tying All Principles Together	133

Foreword

Passion, it is the reason the quarter back plays on with the broken ribs. It is the reason that the gymnast continues the routine knowing that victory may not follow the intense pain. It is the driving force behind so many. It is what made this book possible. An intense desire to see growth in the lives of believers, through prayer.

My friend Nate is himself the product of mercy and truth. A life transformed, now driven by passion to see the lives of others transformed by the same grace that He has come to know. It makes me proud, as one of his spiritual mentors, to see his pioneering spirit in all that he does.

May the reader experience much maturity as they learn to pray. May they get past the ritual and rite, to the very core of communication with the God of Creation. For prayer to be so valuable, so enabling, so rich, few truly know it as the resource that it is. Lack of prayer may be due to many things. For some, it is simply spiritually laziness and apathy. For a few others though, there is desire, overwhelmed inability and possibly ignorance. This book is a light through that darkness. A direct resource! A "how-to" guide to communicating with the God of heaven.

May this book lead you to a deeper and richer relationship with God. May it also, stir in you the passion for God and His kingdom that cannot be quenched in this world!

Now hurry, learn to pray the Bible Way!

Foreword By: Pastor Ryan Bristow

Boaz Church of God - Boaz, Alabama.   Website: www.Boazcog.com

Preface

I have always had a hard time finding the words to say when I pray; especially, when the Pastor would call on me to say the benediction prayer at the end of service. I had a personal prayer life with God. I just didn't think that people in the church would understand my way of praying. I always prayed as though I was really there face to face with God. I talked to Him the same way I would anyone else, but I didn't want the church members to think that I was being disrespectful to God by the way I would speak to Him. There were many times that I would ask God to teach me to pray an out-loud prayer for church. There were things that the Holy Spirit had to show me in the Word of God and in my spirit to help me understand how to pray. One day I was reading a book about prayer and I learned the "Five Principles of Prayer." I never knew that there were principles that I had to follow when I prayed. Shortly after learning the principles of prayer, I realized that they really worked. I then, set out on a conquest through the Bible to find as many principles for prayer as I could! The Word of God is full of principles! It was from that point in my life that I dedicated my life and ministry to searching for lost souls and teaching Christians to pray the Bible way! I pray that you will truly be blessed by this book as your prayer life is transformed and revolutionized into a more glorious life of devotion and dedication to our Lord and Savior, Jesus Christ!

How to Use Your *Teaching*

Christians to Pray the Bible Way

Personal Prayer Journal

Dear Friend,

Take this personal prayer journal and make it your own. Give
it a name. Write your deepest, most precious prayers, and moments
you spend with God inside these covers. Make this a new way to
exercise your faith. Document your prayers to God in this book. Be
persistent in prayer day and night, never ceasing to pray! Document
and date the day that you make mention of your prayer to God and
then wait and watch what God will do for you in your life!
Remember to keep an open mind to God; He works in mysterious
ways, and your answers may not come in a way you expect. When I
asked for wisdom, I didn't receive a divine "poof." I received books.
When you pray, sometimes God will place someone or something in
your life that will enable you to receive what you asked for!

Name Your Personal

Prayer Journal

Give your personal prayer journal a name. Any name is okay.

Example: You can name your journal after biblical characters or after a subject. My personal prayer journal's name is "Blood of the Lamb."

This Journal's Name Is

_____

You can also dedicate this journal to someone:

It Is Dedicated To

_____

You can also honor or remember someone:

In Honor/- Memory Of

_____

Date <u>1-10-10</u>

"And whatever things you ask in prayer, believing, you will receive."

Matthew 21:22

Write Prayer Here:

_____

Lord, I am having a really hard time coping with some problems at work.
Would you give me peace and a victory in this area of my life?

_____

_____

_____

_____

_____

_____

Dear God, thank you for allowing me to speak with you one on one. I want prayer to become more important in my life. I want to develop a more personal prayer life with You! Thank You, Father. Lord I am counting the days until you answer my request, and when You do, I promise to tell everyone how You have heard and answered my prayer! In Jesus name I ask, Amen.

Date <u>2-15-10</u>   God answered my prayer!

Tell now how God answered your request. Did the answer come the way you expected?

_____

_____

The person I was having trouble with at work came up and
_____
apologized to me and even came to church with me this past Sunday!

_____

_____

_____

_____

_____

Dear Lord, I, *(INSERT YOUR NAME)* thank you so much for answering my special prayer request about my troubles at work. Lord, I love You, and I want to tell everyone what you've done for me! Help me Father to grow closer to You through Your Word and through my personal prayer journal as I exercise my faith in a new way by writing my prayers. Lord help me to always put You first in my life. I praise You and lift You up. In Jesus name, Ame

Date _____

"The effectual fervent prayer of a righteous man availeth much"

James 5:16

_____

_____

_____

_____

_____

_____

_____

Dear God, I know that when I pray, You hear me. The verse above says that my prayer will avail much if I am righteous. Help me to be a righteous person in Your sight in all that I do. I ask that You would grant me this request because it means so much to me! Thank You and help me to always be in Your Will in all that I do. In Jesus name I ask, Amen.

Date _____   God answered my prayer!

Tell now how God answered your request. Did the answer come the way you expected?

_____

_____

_____

_____

_____

_____

_____

_____

Dear Lord, You have done it once again! You have answered yet another one of my requests. You are a good God and Father I just want to praise You for what You have done. I promise, Lord, that I will spread Your Word every time I get the opportunity. Thank You and in Jesus name, Amen.

Date _____

"Be joyful always; pray continually; give thanks in all
circumstances, for this is God's Will for you in Christ Jesus"

I Thessalonians 5:16-18

_____

_____

_____

_____

_____

_____

_____

_____

Dear God, I am joyful in my spirit about my prayer today. I'm
really believing in You for a miracle about this! You are still
capable of answering prayers like You did in the Old Testament.
You are still a miracle working God and I need You for a miracle
now Lord! In Jesus name I ask, Amen.

Tell now how God answered your request. Did the answer come the way you expected?

_____

_____

_____

_____

_____

_____

_____

Talk to God here in prayer in your own special way. Talk to Him one on one in your own words and let God bless you with the desires of your heart. Remember to ask in "Jesus name." This is one of the principles for receiving an answer from God through prayer!

Date _____

"When you ask, you do not receive, because you ask with wrong motives, that you may spend what you get on your own pleasures"

James 4:3

_____

_____

_____

_____

_____

_____

_____

_____

Dear God, There have been times in my life Lord when I have asked You for something special and I really believed that You would give it to me and You didn't. I know by (James 4:3) that it is because my motives in prayer were wrong. I wanted to pleasure myself instead of doing what You wanted. Thank You for pointing this out to me Lord. In Jesus name, Amen.

Date _____   God answered my prayer!

Tell now how God answered your request. Did the answer come
the way you expected?

_____

_____

_____

_____

_____

_____

_____

Talk to God here in prayer in your own special way. Talk to Him
one on one in your own words and let God bless you with the
desires of your heart. Remember to ask with the right motives
and not just for your own pleasures. This is one of the principles
for receiving an answer from God through prayer!

Date _____

"And I will do whatever you ask in my name, so that the Son may bring glory to the Father. You may ask me for anything in my name and I will do it"

John 14:13-14

_____

_____

_____

_____

_____

_____

_____

_____

Dear God, You said that You would give me whatever I ask for. Why have I not received an answer to a previous prayer I made mention of to You? Show me Lord what I need to do to receive an answer. In Jesus name I ask, Amen.

Tell now how God answered your request. Did the answer come the way you expected?

_____

_____

_____

_____

_____

_____

_____

_____

Talk to God here in prayer in your own special way. Talk to Him one on one in your own words and let God bless you with the desires of your heart. Remember, I too have also asked God for things in prayer that I have not seen an answer to yet. Be persistent in prayer! This is one of the principles for receiving an answer from God through prayer.

Date _____

"But you, when you pray, enter into your room. And shutting
your door, pray to your Father in secret; and your Father who
sees in secret shall reward you openly"

Matthew 6:6

_____

_____

_____

_____

_____

_____

_____

Dear God, I never realized that I needed to have a secret place in
which to meet with You. I want to develop a secret place in
which to speak with You. Help me to always pray in secret that I
may be rewarded openly! You are amazing Lord and I thank You
and praise You and lift You up Father! In Jesus name I ask,
Amen.

Date _____   God answered my prayer!

Tell now how God answered your request. Did the answer come
the way you expected?

_____

_____

_____

_____

_____

_____

_____

_____

Talk to God here in prayer in your own special way. Talk to Him
one on one in your own words and let God bless you with the
desires of your heart. Remember, when you pray, enter into your
room or your secret place so what you do in secret, God will
reward you openly! This is one of the principles for receiving an
answer from God through prayer.

Date _____

"Bless them that curse you, and pray for them which spitefully use you"

Luke 6:28

_____

_____

_____

_____

_____

_____

_____

Dear God, I have a hard time praying for others that have dome me wrong, but with Your help Lord I know I will overcome. Lord there are times that I knew when people were using me to get what they wanted and then I didn't mean anything else to them. Father, help me not only to pray for them but to forgive them for what they did to me! In Jesus name I ask, Amen.

Date _____   God answered my prayer!

Tell now how God answered your request. Did the answer come
the way you expected?

_____

_____

_____

_____

_____

_____

_____

Talk to God here in prayer in your own special way. Talk to Him
one on one in your own words and let God bless you in ways that
you don't yet understand. Forgiveness is also a principle for
receiving answered prayers!

Walking With God

What's the most awesome prayer that Jesus has ever answered for you? Go to the park or on a nature trail and just spend some quality time with Jesus and thank Him for answered Prayers!

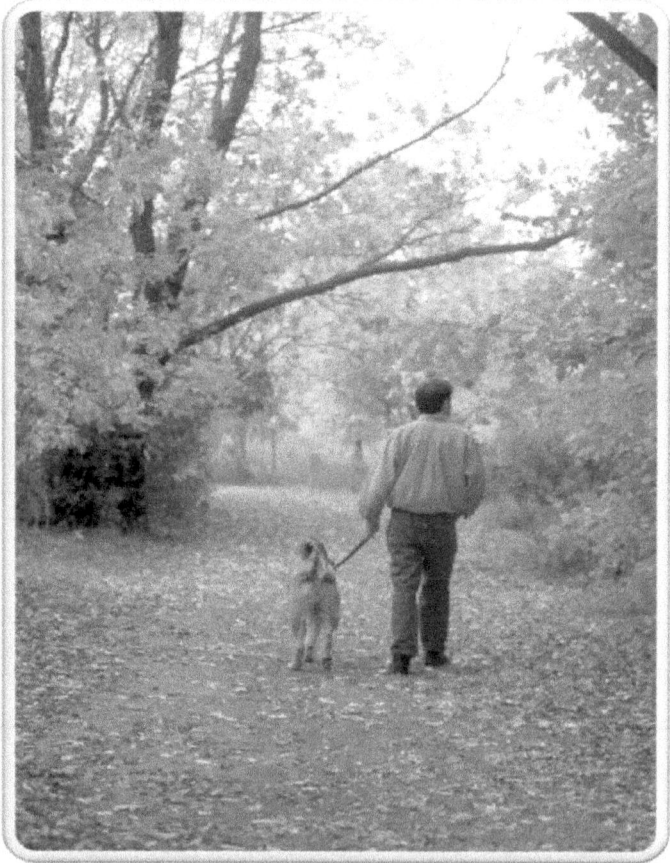

He has shown you, O man, what is good; and what does the Lord require of you? But to do justly, to love mercy, and to walk humbly with God.

Micah 6:8

Relieve Stress…

Take A Prayer Beak!

"Don't worry about anything; instead pray about everything"

Philippians 4:6-7

Speaking from experience today, I want to tell you that you can do all things through Christ who strengthens you! You are an over comer in Jesus name! I used to have anxiety and panic attacks as a teenager. I was constantly stressed out and depressed. I was even sent home from school one time in 10th grade and was told that I needed to go get a drug test performed before I could return back to school. So many times, I felt like the room was spinning around me and I would get dizzy and want to throw up. Constantly, I was worrying about what people thought of me and always accused others of talking about me. The doctors had finally decided to put me on medication. When I moved to Alabama a few years later, I said NO more! I stopped taking all my medications and started praying for deliverance! It's not God's Will for His children to suffer and the Bible says who the Son sets free is free indeed! Jesus set me free and I no longer suffer with these anxiety or panic attacks anymore! Also I'm no longer stressed by the things I used to be stressed by! Of course, I have moments of weakness and I get upset at times from the frustrations of this life, but I'm an over comer in Jesus name!

What are you stressed about today?

Take some time right now and just ask for deliverance! Ask for freedom! Who the Son sets free is free indeed! Jesus doesn't do anything half way! When He says it's over, it's over! When Jesus says be healed, you're healed! When Jesus says be free, your free! When Jesus says it's done, it's done! When Jesus says rise and walk, He means get up and run!!! Praise God today for freedom! I am free today because of Jesus! I no longer suffer from massive amounts of stress! Thank You Jesus!

23 Principles for Receiving

Answered Prayers

1.**Enter His presence with Praise** (Psalm 100:4-5)
2.**Putting God First** (Exodus 20:3)
3.**Daily Prayer** (1 Thess. 5:17)
4.**Forgiveness** (Mark 11:25-26)
5.**Deliverance from Temptation** (Matt. 6:9-13)
6.**Say thank You in advance** (Psalm 50:14)
7.**Being Thankful** (Phil.4:6)
8.**Ask in Jesus name** (John 14:13-14)
9.**Be Specific** (Matt. 21:22)
10.**Ask with the right motives** (John 14:13)
11. **Ask according to God's Will** (1 John 5:14)
12. **Be Persistent** (Eph. 6:18)
13. **Get in the Secret Place** (Matt 6:6)
14. **Fasting** (Isaiah 58)
15. **Trust God** (Prov. 3:5-6)
16. **Wait on the Lord** (Isaiah 40:31)
17. **Honor your mother and father** (Exodus 20:12)
18. **Become a Mountain Mover** (Matt. 17:20)
19. **Don't Fear** (2 Tim. 1:7)
20. **Pray Scripture** (Romans 12:2)
21. **Pray the names of God** (Psalm 91:14)
22. **Beware of vain repetitions** (Matt.6:7)
23.**Believing** (Mark 9:23)

Date _____

"For everyone that asketh, receiveth; and he that seeketh, findeth; and to him that knocketh it shall be opened"

Matthew 7:8

_____

_____

_____

_____

_____

_____

_____

Dear God, I need You more today than ever before for this request. I'm willing to do whatever You need me to do. This verse above says that if I ask, I will receive. Lord I ask You right to move on the prayer I just wrote in this journal! Thank You and I ask it all in Jesus name, Amen.

Date _____   God answered my prayer!

Tell now how God answered your request. Did the answer come the way you expected?

_____

_____

_____

_____

_____

_____

_____

Talk to God here in prayer in your own special way. Talk to Him one on one in your own words and let God bless you in ways your flesh can't stand! Remember to ask in "Jesus name." This is a principle for receiving an answer from God through prayer!

Created To Win!

"We are more than conquerors through Him that loved us"

Romans 8:37

Is there an area of your life that you are struggling with? Whether it be a bad habit, dealing with stress, or learning to forgive someone who did you wrong. Let's pray about it using the principles we have learned so far. Explain below about the struggle you are struggling to overcome.

_____

_____

_____

_____

_____

_____

The Bible says confess your faults one to another so that you may be healed. Find a friend who you can trust and ask them to pray with you over this battle in your life!

"God always answers prayers; the answers may not come in the form you expect or on your time-table, but He always answers. Be careful what you pray for because you just might get more than you asked."

Barbara Eubanks,

Author of Humorous Happenings in Holy Places, And the Angels Laughed, and Laughing with the Lord, A Web Too Tight.

Website: www.BarbaraEubanks.com

Date _____

"He will be very gracious unto thee at the voice of thy cry; when He shall hear it, He will answer thee"

Isaiah 39:19

_____

_____

_____

_____

_____

_____

_____

_____

Dear God, Be gracious unto me; hear my cry as You promised You would. Answer my cry Lord as I also pray today for our nation and our leaders in Washington. Thank You Father, In Jesus name I ask, Amen.

Date _____ God answered my prayer!

Tell now how God answered your request. Did the answer come
the way you expected?

_____

_____

_____

_____

_____

_____

_____

Talk to God again here in your own special way in an out loud
verbal prayer.

If God already knows what I'm going to ask in prayer, before I even ask, than why ask?

Does God really know what we're going to ask?

Some say Yes, some say No, while others say they're not sure. Jesus knows us better then we know ourselves, and He says He knew us before we were born while we were still in the womb. Jesus said He knit us together in our mother's womb. After you've been around a person long enough, you begin to become aware of their attitudes and personalities and it's as though you know what they're going to say before they even open their mouth. Well, you may know what the person will say, but if you and that person don't talk, your personal relationship won't grow. This is why Jesus instructs us to pray even though He already knows what we need. He wants a personal relationship with each and every one of us! So whether or not you believe God knows what you're going to ask, He still desires to communicate with you!

Now think of the most awesome relationship that you share with someone right now. Think of all the fun stuff that the two of you do together. Go ahead and list a few activities below.

1.

2.

3.

4.

5.

Now think of your relationship with Jesus!

Is your relationship with Him as cool as the one you share with your friend? What stuff have you done with Jesus today?

1.

2.

3.

4.

5.

Make an updated prayer list and have it with you when you pray so you can easily remember all the things you want to say to God!

1. Nate Fortner Ministries

2.

3.

4.

5.

6.

7.

8.

9.

10.

11.

12.

13.

14.

15.

Revenge or Forgiveness

"For if ye forgive men their trespasses, your heavenly Father will also forgive you."

Matthew 6:14

The interesting thing about this verse is that it says if we want God to forgive us, then we need to forgive others! So look at it this way. What if we don't forgive others? Does that mean God won't forgive us? Just something to think about the next time you plan revenge.

"But if ye do not forgive, neither will your Father which is in heaven forgive your trespasses."

Mark 11:25-26

So now, here's the hard part. I know you've already got somebody in mind that has hurt you and you need to forgive him/her no matter what happened. This means completely casting your cares upon Jesus and trusting in Him to help make it right!

I want you to pray hard and ask God to help you forgive. Now I want you to forgive that person in your heart, and if at all possible, make the phone call! Even if you weren't the one in the wrong, maybe God's calling you to start the healing process!

This will be hard for some and easy for others. Be prayerful!

Date _____

"And this is the confidence that we have in Him, that, if we ask anything according to His Will, He hears us: And if we know that He hears us, whatsoever we ask, we know that we have the petitions that we desired of Him"

1 John 5:14-15

_____

_____

_____

_____

_____

_____

_____

Dear God, I know that You hear my prayers, because You said so right here in this verse. Lord, answer my prayer and I will praise You and bless Your Holy name. Thank You Father, In Jesus name I ask it, Amen.

Date _____ God answered my prayer!

Tell now how God answered your request. Did the answer come the way you expected?

_____

_____

_____

_____

_____

_____

_____

_____

Talk to God here in prayer in your own special way. Remember that whatsoever you ask, you will receive. Asking according to God's Will is one of the principles for receiving an answer from God through prayer!

Today, I want to challenge you to pray for at least 10 minutes without asking God for anything. Just take time to enter His presence and thank Him for all the prayers He has answered for you. Look back through these pages and thank Him for each prayer He has answered. Even thank Him for the one's He hasn't answered yet. Turn on your praise and worship music as you pray and let the anointing rest on your shoulders all day today! Remember to be thankful for what God has given you. This is one of the principles for receiving an answer from God through Prayer!

List all the dates and prayers that God has answered for you!

<u>Dates</u>   <u>Prayer</u>
<u>Subject</u>

1.

2.

3.

4.

5.

6.

7.

8.

9.

10.

Being one of the most popular verses in the entire Bible, this verse has the most precious promise for anyone who calls on Jesus. Use your knowledge of the scriptures to fill in the missing letters. If you can't figure it out, begin to pray using the principles you've learned so far and ask God to give you guidance as you search through your Bible. If you still need help, call a friend and ask them for help.

F_r God s_ l_v_d the worl_ that He gave His o_ _y
be_o_t_n Son that who_ _ever b_l_e_es in H_m s_o_ld n_t
pe_i_h but   h_ _e ever_asting li_e!

J_ _n 3:_6

The Lord's Prayer

Our Father in heaven

Hallowed be your name.

Your kingdom come.

Your Will be done

On earth as it is in heaven.

Give us this day our daily bread

And forgive us our debts

As we forgive our debtors.

And lead us not into temptation,

But deliver us from evil.

For Yours is the kingdom

And the power

And the glory forever. Amen.

Matthew 6:9-13

911 Prayers

Have you ever had an unexpected accident happen or an emergency arise?

Perhaps while you were driving down the road an animal or child ran out in front of you. You through up a quick Oh help me Jesus! That qualifies as a 911 prayer. Maybe someone calls and gives you the most unexpected news and you say oh Lord help them! That qualifies as a 911 prayer. Have you ever gone into 911 prayer mode?

In this exercise, explain that situation. Tell how it all took place. What was the outcome? Did you learn anything from it? How, if at all, has that situation helped you grow in your relationship with Jesus Christ?

_____

_____

_____

_____

The Day I Prayed For Wisdom

I recall waking up early one morning to the sound of someone talking in my bedroom. As I lied very still trying not to move or draw attention to myself in case it was burglars, I listened very carefully trying to figure out who it was, but I was still sort of sleeping, but awake at the same time. I know it sounds weird that I was awake but sleeping too, but I soon realized that the person talking was me. Yes! I was talking in my sleep. I was praying to God and crying out from the depths of my soul. Matthew 21:22 says "And whatever things you ask for in prayer believing, you will receive." James 1:5 says "If any of you lacks wisdom, let him ask of God, who gives to all liberally and without reproach, and it will be given to him." Well, let me be straight up honest with you! Don't be silly and think that God's just going to drop it into your brain because it doesn't work that way! For the next few minutes, I want to take you on a journey through the deepest parts of my mind so I can show you how my thinking works in case your brain functions the same way mine does and hopefully I'll be able to help you understand a little more how God answers prayer! One time while reading in my Bible I came across where God said if anyone lacks wisdom, then let him pray and ask me for wisdom and I will give it to him. Well I knew from age 12 that God had called me into the ministry and I figured that since I was going to be spending my life working for Jesus that I had better take Him up on that offer of wisdom. So as the days went on, and after much study I asked God, I said "Lord, you said that you would give me wisdom if I asked so Lord Jesus please give me the wisdom I need to run this ministry that you have entrusted to me!" You see, I thought that I was going to receive a Divine poof! I thought that it was going to happen all at once! I thought that I would be driving down the road one day and it would finally hit me and I'd nearly wipe out a tree or two or three parked cars, but I'd finally get the joke that somebody told me a couple of weeks earlier! I was seriously looking for a Divine poof and it never came.

I told God one day, ok, while I'm waiting on you to give me this wisdom you promised me I'm going to get some wisdom on my own. So I started buying a Christian book from Wal-mart each week when I'd get my check. This went on for many weeks, and one day Brandi from the church called and said "Hey Nate, what you doing?" I said "well not much just lying here in the bed watching TV." She said " well Nate, were here at the church packing up some old books that we're giving to the mission and I was just wondering if you would come and help us. Oh and if you see any you want you can have them! I ran out the door and made it to the church within 5 minutes and I picked up a box of books that consisted of about 20-30 books. What a day that was! I was so excited I could hardly sit still. I had to go buy me another book shelf. A few weeks go by and yeah, by this time I am getting wise! I had been reading all these books and I mean I was getting smart! Then guess what happened? I was lying in bed again watching TV and the phone rang. Yep! It was Brandi from the church! She Said "Hey Nate what you doing?" I, trying not to sound lazy said "uh whatever you need me to!" And what she said next was enough to give a young 22 year old preacher a heart attack! "Nate, Pastor Ryan said to give you a call. Somebody has given the church a truck load of books and he said you can have them if you want them!" Brandi then proceeded to ask if I would be driving by the church any time soon. I didn't care if I had to drive through Iraq! Of course I'm coming by the church! This was what I had been praying for! WISDOM!!! I flew to the church and I mean drove really fast breaking every speed limit along the way! When I walked in, oh my goodness there were probably about 15-20 small boxes full of books. Boy and now by this time well I was prospering, I was getting smart! I had to go buy another book shelf! It's funny because most people go shopping looking for the latest hottest item and here I walk in to the store and the greeter says hello sir welcome to Wal-mart I hope you find everything ok, and I say very confidently and proud with a pressed out chest, and in my deepest manliest voice ever "I'm here to buy a bookshelf!" Then they were like uh ok that guy is definitely weird. Well if they thought that was weird they should've been in the bedroom with me a couple of days later when I completely lost it! I work night shift at a local plant and so I sleep during the day. One morning bright and early I hear the voice of someone talking and making noise and I thought how rude man. I worked all night and they're in there making all that noise going to wake me up! So me being noisy as I am, I listened carefully to hear what they were saying and I only heard one voice. After a while I realized that I was crazy, because I had just woke myself up by talking in my sleep! I woke myself up praying! I was asking God for that wisdom He promised me in His Word. "Lord you said!" You know how we as Christians do, always quoting God's own words back to Him. Hey you said! At once the Holy Spirit gripped my heart and my mouth and pretty much said Nate shut up man! You're talking too much! Look around you! Look at that brand new lap top computer. Look at these four bookshelves that are completely full of books! Look at all this WISDOM! It was at that exact moment when it felt as if time had stopped in its tracks, and I realized God had answered my prayer the very day I asked Him for wisdom, but I didn't see it because I was looking for a Divine poof! I learned that day that sometimes when we think God hasn't heard our prayers or that He hasn't answered our prayers, that sometimes we just couldn't see the answer because we were looking for it to come in a specific way and sometimes when God answers a prayer, He equips you with someone or something that will enable you to receive what you asked for in prayer!

What's your wisdom cry?

"If any of you lacks wisdom, let him ask of God, who gives to all liberally and without reproach, and it will be given to him."

James 1:5

Take a few minutes to pray and ask God to provide you with the wisdom you need to carry out the tasks that He has called you to do!

Becoming a Joshua 24:15 Family

As for me and my house, we will serve the Lord.

Joshua 24:15

As I have grown older into adulthood, this verse has become more and more precious to me! Growing up as a child in Huntington, West Virginia, my parents always made sure that my sister Sandra and I went to church. I even remember way back when, when they used to go to church with us. I was never so proud to be with my family as I was on Sunday mornings standing in front of the church at Highlawn Full Gospel Assembly Church with all the other young children looking into the congregation seeing my parents smiling while my sister and I would be singing. What precious memories they are to me! Songs such as Father Abraham, I am a Christian; there is a fountain flowing deep and wide, and many others! Somehow, however, as the years went by though, it seemed that my parents had just lost interest in church. I guess the last time I remember being in church with my family (dad, mom, sister, and myself) was when I first announced my calling to preach at the age of 12. It was a night that I'll never forget. I was preaching on forgiveness. Many of the scriptures I preached that night are still marked in my Bible. Looking back on that memory I imagine how nice it would be if they would have rededicated their lives to the Lord Jesus! My mom had just recently started working night shift at Mariner Health Care of Huntington and that pretty much ruled out the opportunity for her to attend church at all because she would sleep during the day. Every now and then she would stay awake and go with us, but it wasn't every week like we used to as a family.

I also hear many people my age at church who say their so thankful for parents who prayed with them while they were children and growing up. That's another one of those memories I don't have. I don't have those precious memories of times where we as a family would gather and read the Bible or pray. I only have one memory of praying with my mom. It was when my dad was in the army and there was talk about war and my mom grabbed my sister and me at the age of 3 or 4 and she lead us in prayer as we knelt by her bed praying for the safety of my dad. Of course, we had the cute little God is good; God is great prayer over our meals when we were children, but that was a whole other time. What's funny is that my parents always told me that a family that prays together will stay together. I find that funny, because it's so true! I live in Alabama, while my mother and sister are back at home in West Virginia struggling week to week just trying to get by. If you haven't figured it out yet, my parents are now separated. We never prayed together as a family so let this be an example to you! Parents, pray with your children! Love them! Read and study the Bible together with your children!! Don't rob them of those precious memories that they will look back upon once you are gone. What I love so much about Joshua 24:15 is that I declare that when I get married and have children, I will love my wife and children enough to read God's Word to them and pray with them! I grew up in a good home with great parents and with Christian influence and beliefs by my parents. However, when we stopped attending church together as a family, it felt like something inside of me died. My parents were great and still are! I wouldn't be where I am today if it had not been for my parents! Although at times, they couldn't attend church with us, they always made sure that my sister Sandra and I were in church and I'm thankful for that! As for me and my house we will serve the Lord Jesus Christ!!! I want to say thank you mom and dad for always believing in me and always pushing me to do my best! Aim high! Never let anyone still your joy! Dad always said don't let your good be evil spoken of. That's kept me out of a lot of trouble! I believe we are to honor and obey our parents, so with this said, I want the world to know, my parents aren't perfect, but their mine and I love them! I'm not the perfect son, but I know they love me! It is my prayer that one day we will all be back in church serving God together as a family again! I ask that you would join me in praying for my family! Thanks and God Bless!

Take a few minutes here to think about your family.

What precious memories are you providing for your children? Are you reading scripture and praying with them? List below at least 5 things you do with your family that's creating those precious memories! *(For Example: My parents used to take my sister and me all over West Virginia on the weekends to see the caves and waterfalls.)*

1.

2.

3.

4.

5.

Now list at least 5 new memories you would like to create for your family! *(For Example: Reading a Bible story before bed time along with night time prayer.)*

1.

2.

3.

4.

5.

Become a Joshua 24:15 Family!

Date _____

"As for me and my house we will serve the Lord."

Joshua 24:15

_____

_____

_____

_____

_____

_____

_____

Dear God, as for me and my house, we will serve you too! You are the most important person in my life. Help me to be more like You Jesus. You are first and foremost in my life! Lord, I want to leave precious memories for my children. Thank You Jesus and I ask it all in Jesus name, Amen.

Date _____ God answered my prayer!

Tell now how God answered your request. Did the answer come the way you expected?

_____

_____

_____

_____

_____

_____

_____

_____

Talk to God here in prayer in your own special way. The principle here is to put God first as the head of your household. Remember to thank Him for revealing Himself through this principle!

Learn To Pray Scripture

He who dwells in the secret place of the Most High shall abide under the shadow of the Almighty.

Psalm 91:1

Example:

Dear Jesus I want to dwell in the secret place of the Most High where my soul can be filled with joy and peace from above. Lord, I want to abide under your shadow all the days of my life! Oh Almighty God hear my prayer I pray. I'm hungry for more of You and I want to know You more! Thank You Lord and I ask it all in the precious name of Jesus Christ!

Amen.

Every since I was a child, praying at the altar for family prayer time with the adults at Faith Freewill Baptist Church, I would hear them praying through Scripture. What I mean is Pastor Ray Williamson, Bill Plybon, and others such as Rusty Dorton and Tina Tooley would quote Scripture to God when they prayed. Richard and Tammy, and even Charlie Speers would pray this way at times! I always thought that was weird. Why would you tell God what He said? He's the one who wrote the book, I think He knows what it says! I thought wow, that's not very smart! Throw God's Word up in His face, that's a sure way to get what you want! I didn't understand the concept of praying through Scripture and maybe you don't either.

Well, would you like your prayers to be more powerful? Pray the Scriptures! Hebrews 4:12 says that God's Word is alive and powerful, sharper than any two-edged sword. When we speak and pray the Scriptures, we are coming into agreement with God. The Bible also says that the power of life and death are in the tongue. When you start to pray the scriptures, you begin to speak life! Maybe you don't know what to pray in certain situations. 1 John 5:14 tells us we can have confidence in God. Not only does He hear our prayers, but He promises to answer our requests when we pray in line with His Will. Romans 8:26 tells us when we don't know what to pray, the Holy Spirit makes intercession for us. Or in other words, He prays to the

Father on our behalf. Praying the Scripture will increase your Spiritual growth. You can learn what God says about certain situations, and by praying God's Word, you will be praying His Will for your life and you will begin to see your prayers answered! Also this is a great way to memorize Bible verses. O.k., go get your Sunday school memory verse and let's pray that verse. I will show you how with the key verse for my ministry, Acts 2:21.

"And it came to pass that whosoever would call upon the name of the Lord shall be saved." Dear Lord Jesus, Your Word says that whosoever would call on you would be saved! Blessed Jesus I ask that you would allow my Dad to be the next whosoever that calls out your name. Lord I just ask that before it's eternally too late that you would show forth your grace in the lives of the lost in my family. Jesus, I believe that whosoever means anybody and that means that the lost in my family qualify for Salvation. I thank you Jesus for your saving grace and Acts 2:21 for giving me comfort in knowing that you will save my family when they accept you as the Lord of their life! Thank you Father and I ask it in Jesus Name. Amen.

Can you see how by simply adding this verse into my prayer, how I am praying God's Will? The Bible says that God's not willing that any should perish, but that all would come to repentance. So as I prayed and asked Him to save my family, I was agreeing with God. When we pray according to His Will He has promised to answer our request.

"And whatever things you ask in prayer, believing, you will receive."

Matt.21:22

Believing is also a principle for receiving an answer to your prayer! You must believe! Without faith it is impossible to Please God!

Now you try!

Write your memory verse in the space below.

_____

_____

_____

Now in the space provided below, begin to pray through scripture using your memory verse. If you need to, you can look back at my example on the previous page.

_____

_____

_____

_____

_____

Good Job! Now let's take it a step further.

Find two verses to pray through, but instead of just praying those two verses, add some of the previous principles that we've already learned to your prayers from here on out if you haven't already started. You can also pray in the Spirit or in tongues between verses. You can also pray through praise and worship. The Bible says that God inhabits the praises of His people. Have you ever tried to sing your prayer? Have you ever started singing to the Holy Spirit while you're praying? Come into my presence with praise and worship God says! I personally like to play praise and worship music while I pray.

In this exercise, try to use

some of the suggestions I've listed above.

_____

_____

_____

_____

_____

Go ahead and begin to offer Him a song of praise! Begin to sing to Him your favorite song. Even if you don't know any Christian songs, begin to sing your favorite song to Jesus, but do it in an act of worship.

_____

_____

_____

_____

_____

_____

_____

_____

_____

_____

_____

_____

_____

_____

A true Christian is someone who strives hard daily to never let the stress of life, or actions of others ever compromise their faith in God or themselves.

Mark Walker

Stage Coordinator at Whosoever Outreach

Co-Author of "A Look in the Rearview Mirror"

Coming 2014

Today I want to challenge you to pray for at least 10 minutes being persistent in prayer by reminding Jesus of the requests that He hasn't answered yet. Just take time to enter His presence and thank Him for all the prayers He has answered for you. Look back through these pages and thank Him for each prayer He has answered. Even thank Him for the one's He hasn't yet answered. Turn on your praise and worship music as you pray and let the anointing rest on your shoulders all day today! Be specific in your prayer today! This is one of the principles for receiving an answer from God through prayer!

List all the dates and prayers that God hasn't answered for you.

    Date   Prayer Subject

1.

2.

3.

4.

5.

6.

7.

8.

9.

10.

"I can do all things through Christ who strengthens me."

Philippians 4:13

Be sure to tie this verse into your prayer!

_____

_____

_____

_____

_____

_____

_____

_____

Date _____

Be sure to pray this verse in your prayer.

"The fear of the Lord is the beginning of Knowledge, but fools despise wisdom and instruction."

Proverbs 1:7

_____

_____

_____

_____

_____

_____

_____

_____

Date _____

Tell now how God answered your request by praying through scripture. Did the answer come the way you expected?

_____

_____

_____

_____

_____

_____

_____

_____

_____

Lord, I respect you and I tremble in awe at your glory and mercy! Lord I pray that you would touch the hearts of those who despise your wisdom and lead them to the cross. Thank You and I ask in Jesus name. Amen.

Date _____

Be sure to pray this verse in your prayer.

"In the last days I will pour out my Spirit upon all flesh."

Joel 2:28

_____

_____

_____

_____

_____

_____

_____

_____

_____

Date _____

Tell now how God answered your request by praying through scripture. Did the answer come the way you expected?

_____

_____

_____

_____

_____

_____

_____

_____

Lord, let Your Spirit fall upon me as I desire to grow closer to You in prayer through this book. I ask that you would touch the lives of everyone who opens the pages of Teaching Christians to pray the Bible Way! I ask in Jesus name, Amen.

Date _____

Be sure to pray this verse in your prayer.

"Wealth gained by dishonesty will be diminished, but he who gathers by labor will increase."

Proverbs 13:11

_____

_____

_____

_____

_____

_____

_____

_____

Date _____

Tell now how God answered your request by praying through scripture. Did the answer come the way you expected?

_____

_____

_____

_____

_____

_____

_____

_____

Lord, help me in all my ways to be honest. I know a man who doesn't work, doesn't eat. Lord, I declare that I will be honest! I will lead by example for my children. In Jesus name, Amen.

Date _____

Be sure to pray this verse in your prayer.

"Therefore, if anyone is in Christ, he is a new creation; old things have passed away; behold all things have become new."

2 Corinthians 5:17

_____

_____

_____

_____

_____

_____

_____

_____

_____

Date _____

Tell now how God answered your request by praying through scripture. Did the answer come the way you expected?

_____

_____

_____

_____

_____

_____

_____

_____

Now take some time to pray in your own words in an out loud prayer to God. Also remember to keep using the principles from the previous chapters.

Over the next few pages, fill in your own verses to use in your prayers.

I CAN DO ALL THINGS THROUGH CHRIST WHO STRENGTHNS ME.

Philippians 4:13

Lord I know I struggle from time to time, but I know I can do all things through Jesus who gives me strength all day long!

Amen.

_____

_____

_____

_____

                        _____

_____

_____

_____

_____

_____

_____

_____

Amen.

_____

_____

_____

_____

                    _____

_____

_____

_____

_____

_____

_____

Amen.

_____

_____

_____

_____

                    _____

_____

_____

_____

_____

_____

_____

                              Amen.

_____

_____

_____

_____

                              _____

_____

_____

_____

_____

_____

_____

_____

_____

                                        Amen.

Amen.

_____

_____

_____

_____

                    _____

_____

_____

_____

_____

_____

_____

                                   Amen.

Amen.

"Prayer is more than a wish list we say to God, it is the privilege of having a conversation with the Father who made us, the Savior who redeemed us, and the Holy Spirit who empowers us."

-Harry Whitt

-Founder of Pathway Outreach Ministries, Inc.est.1994

Sardis, Alabama www.PathwayOutreach.org

Now let's take it a step farther by praying through two verses and add as many of the principles as possible from the previous chapters. This will be an out loud prayer.

1. _____

_____

_____

2. _____

_____

_____

What principles are you going to use in your prayer?

1. Enter His presence with praise
2. Putting God first
3. Daily Prayer
4. Forgiveness
5. Saying thank You in advance
6. Being Thankful
7. Ask in Jesus name
8. Be specific
9. Ask with the right motives
10. Get in the Secret Place

Prayer Poem

Take time in this exercise to write out a prayer poem. The Psalms are a collection of poetry and prayers, most of which were written by David. Remember, David was a man after God's own heart, so take a moment here to write your love song to Jesus!

Give your prayer a nice title.

                                                Prayer Title

_____

_____

_____

_____

_____

_____

_____

_____

_____

Intercessory Prayer

Denying self to seek God's Will for

someone else's life.

-Nate Fortner

Prayer List

Let's make an updated prayer list to pray over. Here are some suggestions: The persecuted church, government officials, your Pastor, family, and friends.

1.

2.

3,

4.

5.

6.

7.

8.

9.

10.

11.

12.

13.

The Bible says:

Jesus is seated at the right hand of the Father making intercession for us. When we pray, Jesus prays to the Father on our behalf telling Him what it is that we need. When we make intercession for someone, we are praying on behalf of the person we are praying for. However, when you know you need to pray and you don't know what to pray, the Bible says in Romans 8:26 "likewise the Spirit also helps in our weakness. For we do not know what to pray as we ought, but the Spirit Himself makes intercession for us with groaning which cannot be uttered."

I don't know what type of prayer could possibly be any more powerful than intercessory prayer. In intercessory prayer, you're denying self to pray for someone else's needs and desires, and when you don't know what to pray, the Holy Spirit will pray for you! Go ahead and grab your new prayer list and begin to intercede on behalf of those people!

You can't expect them to pray in the school house until they pray in the church house, and you can't expect them to pray in the White House until we first pray in the church house!

Pastor Tommy Bates

Community Family Church

Independence, Kentucky

www.TommyBates.com

Coffee Break With Jesus

Alright, today let's go out for coffee! Pick a coffee shop, any coffee shop! The key to this exercise is to get out of the house. You can also ask a friend to go with you if you want. So many of us are cool with Jesus at church or at home when we need Him. We usually call on Him in the bad times, but we should also call upon Him in the good times too! In Matthew 18:20, Jesus said "For where two or three are gathered together in my name, I am in the midst of them." Let Jesus join you for coffee today! Go fellowship with a friend and begin to tell them how good God has been to you, and Jesus will show up and be in the midst with you! To acknowledge His presence, you could even add a chair for Him to sit. When we begin to become aware of His presence, we will begin to see our prayers answered. We will begin to see miracles. We will begin to take our relationship to the next level!

When you get back from the coffee shop, in the space provided below, describe the experience you had by acknowledging Jesus' presence! Did you pull up a chair for Him to sit in? To some, pulling up a chair may seem childish, but Jesus said in Mark 10:14-15 "Let the children come to me, and do not forbid them; for of such is the kingdom of God. Assuredly, I say to you, whoever does not receive the kingdom of God as a little child will by no means enter it." Sometimes, what may seem childish to man is faith to God! "Without faith it is impossible to please God." Hebrews 11:6.

Take a few minutes to describe your experience at the coffee shop today and how that has deepened your prayer life or how it didn't.

_____

_____

_____

_____

_____

_____

_____

Praying the Names of God

Until you know Jesus as Savior, you can't call Him Savior! Until you know Him as provider, You can't call Him Jehovah-Jireh? Until you've seen His healing power, how can you call Jesus Jehovah-Rapha? Until you know Jesus for who He is, you only have a preconceived imagination of God or what you've heard others say about Him! In this chapter, I want to help you grow closer to Jesus by knowing Him by name and the authority you have to use His name! In this section, I list 20 names of God. Some I will elaborate on more than others because I know Him personally by those names!

NAME OF GOD	MEANING
1. Adonai	The Lord My Great Lord
2. EL	The Strong One
3. EL Elohe Yisrael	God, The God of Israel
4. Elohim	The All-Powerful One Creator
5. El Olam	The Eternal God, The Everlasting God
6. El Roi	The God who sees me
7. El Shaddai	The All Sufficient One, The God Of the mountains, God Almighty
8. Immanuel	God with us
9. Jehovah	I AM, The One who is the self- existent one
10. Jehovah-Jireh	The Lord my provider
11. Jehovah-Meaddishkem	The Lord who sanctifies
12. Jehovah-Nissi	The Lord is my Banner
13. Jehovah-Rapha	The Lord who heals
14. Jehovah-Rohi	The Lord is my shepherd
15. Jehovah-Sabaoth	The Lord of Hosts, The Lord of Armies
16. Jehovah-Shalom	The Lord of Peace
17. Jehovah-Shammah Companion	The Lord is there, The Lord is my
18. Jehovah-Tsidkenu	The Lord our Righteousness
19. Yahweh	The Self-Existent One
20. Yeshua	Jesus

Immanuel—God with us— is always reassuring to me because at those moments in my life when it seems that nobody cares and that I'm all alone, Jesus is with me! He loves me and cares for me. Jeremiah 29:11 says "For I know the thoughts that I think toward you, says the LORD, thoughts of peace and not of evil, to give you a future and a hope." It seems that I can always find a friend in Jesus!

Jehovah-Jireh-the Lord my provider- the first time I ever remember hearing the name Jehovah was when I heard the name Jehovah-Jireh. Just as God provided a ram as a substitute for Isaac, He provided a lamb (His Son Jesus) as the ultimate sacrifice! God will meet all our needs. Jesus has provided everything that I'll ever need. Money, a truck, a computer, a loving family and I'm so thankful for all my friends and church family! I may not own a mansion or have lots of money, but I'm a millionaire in faith and hope and love and I've got more than my share! I'm blessed! All good things come from above!

Jehovah-Rohi— The Lord is my shepherd— In the Bible, Christians are compared to sheep that need a shepherd. Psalm 23 says it like this:

The Lord is my Shepherd; I shall not want. He maketh me to lie down in green pastures: He leadeth me beside the still waters. He restoreth my soul: He leadeth me in the paths of righteousness for His name's sake. Yea, though I walk in the valley of the shadow of death, I will fear no evil: for thou art with me; thy rod and thy staff they comfort me. Thou preparest a table before me in the presence of mine enemies: thou anointest my head with oil; my cup runneth over. Surely goodness and mercy shall follow me all the days of my life: and I will dwell in the house of the Lord forever. When I feel lost and miserable, and I have no direction, I pray Jehovah-Rohi lead me by the still waters, speak sweet peace to my soul! Daystar shine down on me! Lead me Lord and I'll follow!

Yeshua-Jesus– While watching the film The Passion of the Christ, I heard the Pharisee's at multiple times call Jesus Yeshua. Then I began to hear local and TV preachers refer to Jesus as Yeshua. Yeshua is the Hebrew translation for Jesus. So now when I pray, I like to say Yeshua at times.

Now that you know some of the names of God and what they mean to me, study these names and see which names you know God by. Are there any of these names that you can relate to Him with, such as Jehovah-Shalom the Lord is my peace? Has God spoken peace to your soul when you were in despair? Were you in the middle of the biggest turmoil of your life? Perhaps you know Him as healer. Has Jehovah recently healed you of a sickness or disease such as cancer or diabetes? If so, then when you pray, refer to Him as Jehovah-Rapha. Start praying to Him as healer! Maybe you're sick now and you've been back and forth to the doctor and you're still sick. Start praying to The Great Physician named Jesus! Pray as if you believe He can and that He will heal you! When you pray for healing, try calling Him Jehovah-Rapha. Expand your prayer life and your relationship with Christ by calling Him by name! Let me lead you in prayer!

Dear Jesus, I thank you for being Immanuel– God with us. Thank you for coming to this earth to die for my sin. Your Word says that by your stripes we were healed. Because I know you as healer, I can truly call you Jehovah-Rapha! When I was sick, you healed my body. Jehovah-Rohi, you are my shepherd. You lead me in the paths of righteousness. El Shaddai, you are God Almighty! Jehovah-Shammah, you are my companion who goes with me and I'm never alone. I always have you to share in the good times and in the bad times! Yeshua, I love you and I can't express with words the joy I feel in my heart. Thank you for saving me! In Jesus name, Amen.

Now you try it. In the space provided, use the names of God. In this exercise, you will deepen your faith, your prayer life, and grow closer in your relationship with Jesus Christ!

Dear God, I'm so excited that I can know you by name. Jehovah-Rapha, you are my healer. When I thought that my prayer life would never deepen, it has today, because I know that you are Yahweh, the Self-_____ One! Jehovah, when my _____ was in the military, you were Jehovah-Sabaoth, the Lord of _____ Armies. You are my Banner. Elohim, you are the All Powerful Lord of my life. Thank you and I ask in Yeshua's name. Amen.

Over the next few pages, use the names of God as you pray throughout this section of your journal, but remember to continue to use the principles you've already learned in the previous chapters.

What's the name of your church?

_____

What's your Pastor's name?

_____

What's your Pastor's wife's name?

_____

What's your worship leader's name?

_____

List below any others in leadership in your church.

1.

2.

3.

4.

5.

In this prayer, use the names of God to intercede for your church
and the leadership in your church. Pray that God's Will is done in
their lives of the people in the church. This prayer is an out loud
prayer. Don't write this one. Take it right off the top of your
head. If you need to, refer to the list of the names for God.

Date _____

Jehovah-Jireh

_____

_____

_____

_____

_____

_____

_____

_____

_____

_____

_____

_____

_____

_____

_____

Date _____

Tell now how God answered your request. How do you feel calling God by name helped you to receive an answer to your prayer? Did the answer come the way you expected?

_____

_____

_____

_____

_____

_____

_____

_____

_____

_____

_____

_____

Dear Lord, I pray that the one reading this book will begin to grow closer to you in their prayer life! I pray that you would just begin to reveal Yourself more and more to them through Your wonderful many different names. I ask this in Jesus precious Holy name, Amen.

Date _____

Jehovah-Tsidkenu

_____

_____

_____

_____

_____

_____

_____

_____

_____

_____

_____

_____

_____

_____

_____

Date _____

Tell now how God answered your request. How do you feel calling God by name helped you to receive an answer to your prayer? Did the answer come the way you expected?

_____

_____

_____

_____

_____

_____

_____

_____

_____

_____

_____

Jehovah, I praise You! Elohim, you're all powerful. El Shaddai, You are all sufficient! Jesus, You are Jehovah-Meaddishkem. Sanctify me Yeshua! Oh Jesus You're awesome! Amen.

Date _____

Jehovah-Nissi

_____

_____

_____

_____

_____

_____

_____

_____

_____

_____

_____

_____

Date _____

Tell now how God answered your request. How do you feel calling God by name helped you to receive and answer to your prayer? Did the answer come the way you expected?

_____

_____

_____

_____

_____

_____

_____

_____

_____

_____

_____

Jehovah, I praise You! Jehovah-Nissi You are my Banner! You lead me in battle Jehovah-Sabaoth. Oh, Immanuel, You are with me. I know you hear me when I call. Thank You in advance for the miracles and blessings I know I will see in the future. In Jesus name I ask, Amen.

Date _____

Jehovah-Rohi

_____

_____

_____

_____

_____

_____

_____

_____

_____

_____

_____

_____

Date _____

Tell now how God answered your request. How do you feel calling God by name helped you to receive an answer to your prayer? Did the answer come the way you expected?

_____

_____

_____

_____

_____

_____

_____

_____

_____

_____

_____

_____

Jehovah, I praise You! Jehovah-Rohi, You are my Shepherd. Lead me Lord and I will follow anywhere You open up the door! Lord I pray that You would allow me to grow even more closer to You. In Jesus name I ask, Amen.

Date _____

Yahweh

_____

_____

_____

_____

_____

_____

_____

_____

_____

_____

_____

_____

Date _____

Tell now how God answered your request. How do you feel calling God by name helped you to receive an answer to your prayer? Did the answer come the way you expected?

_____

_____

_____

_____

_____

_____

_____

_____

_____

_____

_____

_____

Jehovah, I praise You! Yahweh, I'm so glad that the faith of others in You doesn't depend upon me. So many times, I feel like I've let You down, but Lord You are great and mighty and awesome in power! You are Yahweh; the Self-Existent One! I love You Yeshua and I ask it all in Jesus name.

Date _____

Adonai

_____

_____

_____

_____

_____

_____

_____

_____

_____

_____

_____

_____

_____

Date _____

Tell now how God answered your request. How do you feel calling God by name helped you to receive an answer to your prayer? Did the answer come the way you expected?

_____

_____

_____

_____

_____

_____

_____

_____

_____

_____

_____

_____

Adonai, I give You praise! Great in glory, Great in honor! Great in Glory! Jesus, You are my great God! Thank You for Your love. In Jesus name I ask, Amen.

Date _____

El Shaddai

_____

_____

_____

_____

_____

_____

_____

_____

_____

_____

_____

_____

Date _____

Tell now how God answered your request. How do you feel calling God by name helped you to receive an answer to your prayer? Did the answer come the way you expected?

_____

_____

_____

_____

_____

_____

_____

_____

_____

_____

_____

_____

Yahweh, I praise You! You are El Shaddai, the All Sufficient One. You are the God of the mountains. You are! Yes, Lord, You are everything to me! You, You, You! In Jesus name, Amen.

Date _____

Jehovah-Rapha

_____

_____

_____

_____

_____

_____

_____

_____

_____

_____

_____

_____

Date _____

Tell now how God answered your request. How do you feel calling God by name helped you to receive an answer to your prayer? Did the answer come the way you expected?

_____

_____

_____

_____

_____

_____

_____

_____

_____

_____

_____

_____

_____

Jehovah, I praise You! Jehovah-Rapha, I believe You're my healer! I believe You're more than enough for me! I believe You're my strength! Jesus, You're my all in all. In Jesus name I pray, Amen.

Date _____

Choose a name for God that you would like to pray.

_____
Name of God

_____

_____

_____

_____

_____

_____

_____

_____

_____

_____

_____

_____

Date _____

Tell now how God answered your request. How do you feel calling God by name helped you to receive an answer to your prayer? Did the answer come the way you expected?

_____

_____

_____

_____

_____

_____

_____

_____

_____

_____

_____

_____

_____

Today, call a friend and tell them you are nearing the end of this book and you wanted to pray with them. I challenge you that as you do this today, that you will give them a copy of this book as a gift so they too can grow closer to Jesus in their prayer life!

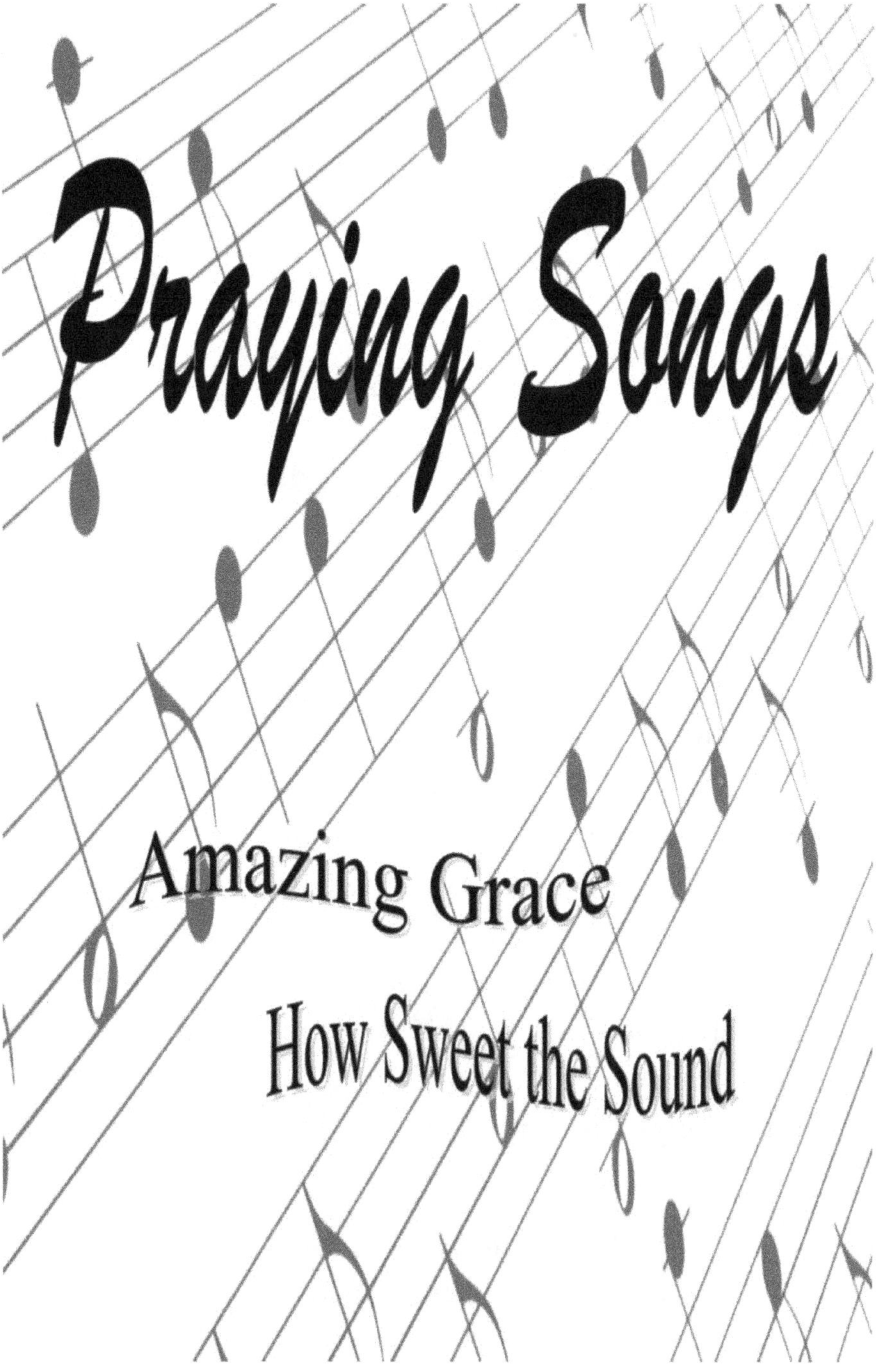
Praying Songs
Amazing Grace
How Sweet the Sound

Praying Songs

In the English language, when we speak of worshipping God, we usually use words like praise and worship. Have you ever given much thought to what praise and worship really means? Webster defines praise as to glorify, express approval or admiration of. The word worship is defined as this: reverence, adoration, adore: love and admire, but what do each of these words mean? For example, let's look at the word adore. Webster says the word adore means worship, love intensely, and pray to. In my study of the words, I found that many of the definitions mostly all meant the same thing. However, in the Hebrew each act of worship is defined by its own word.

If I didn't know how to worship and I studied words to see how to worship, then there's no definition to show you how. In the Church we raise our hands, sing, cry, bow our heads and some even shout, but where is it written that that's how to worship? Nevertheless, I wanted to know more about how to worship God. I had questions like, why do we worship the way we do or how can I worship in a way pleasing to God? In the English language, we can say praise and worship and it covers all styles of worship, but in the Hebrew there are names given to each style of worship.

The first one I want to speak about is "Halal" which is a hilarious praise. The hilarious praise is in those moments when people are so full of the joy of the Spirit that they just smile and laugh.

Second, there is the word "Yadah" which is to raise your hands toward heaven. "Barak" means to kneel down and worship. My favorite is the Hebrew word "Shabach" which means to shout with a voice of triumph! There have been many times while preaching in a Church that I would shout the word Shabach and the congregation would shout their praise unto God. "Zamar" means to play instruments. We see many times in Psalms where God says play songs on the stringed instruments. God is a God of music, and so it's for this reason I had to add this newest chapter, Praying Songs.

The word "Tehillah" basically means your testimony in song. As Christians, we all have a story to tell. We all have a testimony. Each of us have our own song or Tehillah praise to offer to the Lord.

Many times while at home alone, I find myself singing out loud a song of praise. It starts off small and quiet in my heart, but it gracefully reaches my vocal chords and pushes out of my mouth and Jesus is glorified. With my voice I can sing different musical notes such as G, F, or C. In the same way, a guitar or stringed instrument can do the same. So in a way, we as Christians are walking, talking, breathing instruments of praise unto God everywhere we go!

I started singing some Tehillah praise at work one day and I just kept getting louder and louder until I had the other associates listening. It went like this:

"How can I embrace the thought of your grace when I can't look past the thought of my disgrace? I'm a sinner and I know that I am, but in Your hands Jesus, I know who I am! I'm saved. I'm a child of the King! There's royal blood flowing through my veins and one day soon with You I'll reign!"

It's though Tehillah praise that I've written hundreds of songs, but only managed to get a few written down on paper. I wonder how many songs we listen to on the Christian radio stations are really the product of Tehillah Praise?

Psalm 95:6-7 says, "O come let us worship and bow down: let us kneel before the Lord our maker. For He is our God, and we are the people of His pasture, and the sheep of His hand. Today if you will hear His voice." In this verse I immediately recognize "Barak" praise because it says to kneel down. What other praise words can you find in this verse? What songs come to mind when you think of "Barak" praise?

In my mind, I wonder how songwriters feel as they're writing their songs. Do the words come easily and flow right along or is it difficult sometimes? I imagine it could be both ways, but I wonder if they ever experience the cradling of the Holy Spirit as they worship and write. Sometimes when I hear songs like *"Amazing Grace My Chains Are Gone"* by Chris Tomlin, I want to Shabach and Barak at the same time because I'm reminded that in Jesus I'm free! Big Daddy Weave gets me every morning in the truck on the way to work with *"I Am Redeemed."* Then I escape to that Secret Place within and all I can do it Barak and make an altar in my heart to offer my sacrifice of praise.

I've caught myself many times at work praying and then all of a sudden I'm halfway through a song and the Holy Spirit comes on me and I get a good ole dose of the Holy Ghost! I wipe away the tears of joy and just keep working praising God throughout the day.

Over the next few pages, I want you to journal your prayers like you have throughout the whole book, except this time, not only will you be writing and speaking your prayers, but you will be worshipping by exercising the Hebrew descriptions for praise. In your prayer, you could Shabach, Barak, Towdah, or even sing some Tehillah praise unto God. This exercise is not for show, but to help you to see that there are many different ways to worship. When we worship, we must worship in Spirit and in Truth!

Hebrew Words for Praise

1. **Halal / לאלח** - a hilarious praise.
2. **Yadah** - to raise your hands up to heaven.
3. **Towdah** – to raise your hand in giving thanks.
4. **Shabach / חבאש** - to shout loud with a voice of triumph.
5. **Barak / קרב** – to kneel down and worship.
6. **Zamar / ראמאז** – to play instruments.
7. **Tehillah / הליהת** – Your testimony in song.

Date: _____

Halal

_____

_____

_____

_____

_____

_____

_____

_____

_____

_____

_____

_____

Date: _____

Tell now how God answered your request. How do you feel that your worship experience was enhanced when you prayed with Halal praise?

_____

_____

_____

_____

_____

_____

_____

_____

_____

_____

Jehovah, Your Word says where two agree as touching anything that it would be given to them. Jehovah-Jireh I come into agreement with the reader right now that their prayer would be answered in Jesus' Mighty name!

Date: _____

Yadah

_____

_____

_____

_____

_____

_____

_____

_____

_____

_____

_____

Date: _____

Tell now how God answered your request. How do you feel that your worship experience was enhanced when you prayed with Yadah praise?

_____

_____

_____

_____

_____

_____

_____

_____

_____

_____

_____

Jesus, I thank you for helping me to learn the different ways to praise You! I pray that I will continue to learn how to bring you glory! In Jesus name, Amen.

Date: _____

Towdah

_____

_____

_____

_____

_____

_____

_____

_____

_____

_____

_____

Date:_____

Tell now how God answered your request. How do you feel that your worship experience was enhanced when you prayed with Towdah praise?

_____

_____

_____

_____

_____

_____

_____

_____

_____

_____

_____

_____

Dear Jehovah- Nissi, I thank you with Towdah praise as I raise my hands to You! I love You and I know you have declared my end from the beginning.

Date: _____

Shabach

_____

_____

_____

_____

_____

_____

_____

_____

_____

_____

Date: _____

Tell now how God answered your request. How do you feel that your worship experience was enhanced when you prayed with Shabach praise?

_____

_____

_____

_____

_____

_____

_____

_____

_____

_____

_____

Whoa! Glory to God in the Highest! You are worthy of the highest praise! I will shout praises from the mountain tops and even in the valleys low!

Date: _____

Barak

_____

_____

_____

_____

_____

_____

_____

_____

_____

_____

_____

Date: _____

Tell now how God answered your request. How do you feel that your worship experience was enhanced when you prayed with Barak praise?

_____

_____

_____

_____

_____

_____

_____

_____

_____

_____

_____

I kneel down before you Lord Jesus and give You everything that I am. I am nothing without You Lord. I pray that You will help me to grow closer to You every day!

Date:_____

Zamar

_____

_____

_____

_____

_____

_____

_____

_____

_____

_____

_____

Date: _____

Tell now how God answered your request. How do you feel that your worship experience was enhanced when you prayed with Zamar praise?

_____

_____

_____

_____

_____

_____

_____

_____

_____

_____

_____

I will praise You with Zamar! I will play an instrument for Your enjoyment Father, and when I have no stringed instrument to play then I will sing with my voice!

Date: _____

Tehillah

_____

_____

_____

_____

_____

_____

_____

_____

_____

_____

Date: _____

Tell now how God answered your request. How do you feel that your worship experience was enhanced when you prayed with Tehillah praise?

_____

_____

_____

_____

_____

_____

_____

_____

_____

_____

_____

_____

I lift my voice with praise on my tongue that no fiery dart of the enemy can extinguish! My life is Yours and I live to be a blessing unto You Jesus! Walk with me Lord as I strive to walk with You each day as a reflection of Your marvelous light of grace!

What's your testimony in song sound like?

What has God brought you through recently? Did you overcome an issue at school, with a friend, or a family member? In this exercise, I want you to begin to sing and write it down so that you'll always have it to look back on. For example, your Tehillah praise could sound and read as follows:

Lord, I know that you've brought me through the deepest darkest sins of my past. It's in You that I find peace and the strength to carry on. It's in You that I live and grow closer to You Jesus every day! It's in You that forever I will remain. You saw me through all my failures and falls, but in my heart, from Your love, I'll never fall!

As you sing your Tehillah praise, you can make it up the tune as you go. It's okay if you feel you're not a singer and can't carry a tune in a bucket because Jesus loves to hear you sing. Even if it is only in the shower or in the car, Jesus still loves to hear you sing! Lift up your voice in praise to the Father right now! Let God bless you in a way like never before as you sing to Him!

Just in case you didn't know, God likes to sing too! He sings over you when you don't even know it! Zephaniah 3:17 says "The Lord thy God in the midst of thee is mighty; He will save. He will rejoice over thee with joy. He will rest in His love. He will joy over thee with singing." Doesn't it make you wonder what God's favorite song is? Maybe it's the one you wrote or are getting ready to write? It's the song of the redeemed!

That's any song you sing that brings Him glory! Are you willing to sing a duet tonight with God? When you start sending up praise, He'll start to joy over you while He starts singing! I can imagine right now that tonight in your house heaven will be meeting earth right there in your prayer closet! Below take time if you can to pen some lyrics to the page.

_____

_____

_____

_____

_____

_____

_____

_____

_____

_____

_____

_____

I believe if we as Christians would worship God the way He deserves to be worshipped, then I believe we could see Revival come to America! Too many of us focus on the bad things that happen and we forget that our God is a Great Big God! I hear Christians and non-Christians both complain all the time that this country has fallen so far and is on the verge of judgment! My question though is this: What are we doing to make a difference?

2 Chronicles 7:14-15 says "If My people who are called by My name will humble themselves, and pray and seek My face, and turn from their wicked ways, then I will hear from heaven, and I will forgive their sin and heal their land. Now my eyes will be open and My ears attentive to prayer made in this place." It just takes one person to make a big difference! I think we need to remember today that no matter what the circumstance, the greatest victory always follows the greatest battle! I've said it before and I'll say it again, "If your Bible's not falling apart then your life probably is!"

I pray that today you will decide to walk closer with Jesus Christ in every aspect of your life. I pray that as you have stepped out in faith and written your prayers in this journal that your prayer life will never be the same. I trust by now that you have established a Prayer Closet where you can meet with Yeshua every single day! I pray for you the reader that you will always have a passion to know Jesus more!

Submit your prayer request to:
NateFortnerMinistries@yahoo.com so I can personally pray over your specific needs when I go into my Prayer Closet! May God Bless you mightily!

It is my most heartfelt prayer for you that your prayer life is revolutionized!

Tying All Prayer Principles Together

In this chapter, I want to tie in all the principles from the previous chapters. I want to really lead you in a powerful prayer here! Use as many principles as you can. Remember to enter your secret prayer place, whether it's your bedroom, a clothes closet, your bathroom or where ever you pray most often! Turn your praise and worship music on and get ready for a time of prayer like you've never experienced before! This is time for just you and God to commune as I lead you in prayer. The Bible says when we're saved, we receive the Holy Spirit and where two or more are gathered in Jesus' name, He would be in the midst of them. We also know from the Bible that there are guardian angels that are with us. If you didn't know it before, let me now tell you, there is a heavenly host with you at all times and even right now they are there surrounding you with the love of Jesus and the Bible says whatsoever things you ask in prayer, you will receive!

Let's Pray!!!

Dear Jesus,

I worship you Lord by putting you first today. I desire to grow closer to you through daily prayer. Lord, I also ask that you would forgive me Jesus of any sins that I may have in my life right now so that my prayer is not hindered. Jehovah, I pray that you would deliver me from the temptations of sin, and I thank you in advance Lord for what you've done in my prayer life! I am so thankful Yeshua for all you have done for me! I thank you for loving me so much that you would come and die on the cross for me! Jehovah-Jireh I pray in Jesus name today as I ask that you would touch the lives of the lost in my family and friends. I also ask that you would touch the lives of the lost in Nate's family. Yahweh, I know it's not your will that any should perish, but that all would come to repentance. This is how I know that the lost in my family will be saved. I'm confident in Christ! Lord I call upon you today from my secret place and I worship you for you are Holy! Holy! Holy! Holy!

Go ahead and begin to pray in your own words for a little while, you can do it! Philippians 4:13 says you can! Turn your worship CD up and praise, and sing and pray, and worship, and dance like David danced if you want!

Lord your Word says in Romans 8:37 that we are more than conquerors through Him that loved us. Your

prosper! Lord your Word is a lamp to my feet and a light for my path. I don't have enough words to praise you with Lord. You are beyond my ability to understand or express. Jehovah-Nissi, I just raise my hands in worship. Psalm 95:6-7 says "O come, let us worship and bow down: let us kneel before the Lord our maker. For He is our God; and we are the people of His pasture, and the Sheep of His hand." I kneel and worship you Jesus! Jesus! Savior! Redeemer! Alpha and Omega! Beginning and the End! Light of the World! John 4:24 says that God is a Spirit: and they that worship must worship in spirit and in truth! El Shaddai, I fall on my face just at the mention of your Holy name! I cry Holy! Hallelujah! Hallelujah! Glory to the Lamb of God! To the glory of your name Jesus, you died just to save us! Your blood poured out for me. When it should have been me to die on that cross for the punishment of my own sin, Wow! But your mercy said No! Mercy and goodness showed up to plead my case and even in my guilty condition, You still loved me!

Go ahead and begin to pray in your own words as I take time right now to enter my secret place to pray for you, the reader of this book! It is my prayer that as we come to the end of this book that I have been able to help you in your prayer life! Ultimately, all praise and Honor go to Jesus Christ! I pray a very special blessing upon you and your life that you will always continue to follow hard after Jesus! He loves you and cares for you more then you'll ever know!

Oh Jehovah God! Jehovah Jesus! I pray that you would supernaturally touch the person who has just finished ready this book. Lord I pray that you would be an ever present help to them in their life! Savior, I pray that you would give them the desires of their heart as they trust you with their every waking breath! Hallelujah! Redeemer! I pray that their prayer life just doesn't wither away now that this book has come to an end! Lord I ask on behalf of this person, that you would lead and guide them to another book on prayer! Help them to go even further in their prayer life! Thank you Jesus for this person reading this book: "Teaching Christians to Pray the Bible Way." and I ask it all in Jesus name.

Amen.

In Conclusion

(A personal message from Nate)

It has been an awesome journey for me over the past two years as I have embarked on the journey of writing this book! Since I have moved to Alabama, God has just done a work in my life like I never thought would have even been possible! However, just so you know, it wasn't all that easy! When I first moved to Alabama, that was my first taste of real freedom from my parents and I went a little wild. I spent many mornings waking up praying and thanking God that I had made it home from the party the night before! Life hasn't been easy, but it's been easier since I let Jesus back in. There were times that I knew God was dealing with my heart to get right and so I would try to please Him enough to get Him off my back. I remember numerous times I would party all night and go to church Sunday morning with the biggest hang over ever! Trust me, that's not cool, because then strong conviction sets in! On the other hand, I thank Jesus for saving my soul! I'm so glad that I serve the God of second chances! I am currently involved in leadership in my church; I am the Founder of Whosoever Outreach and Nate Fortner Ministries. My life has been blessed! I am going to be praying over these books and believing God for miracles in the lives of the readers! It is my deepest prayer that you learn to pray and grow in your relationship with Jesus. I hope that some way, somehow that this book has been a blessing to you. If you don't go to church, then get involved in a good Bible believing church and learn everything about God that you can. He is a friend that will never fail you! He will never leave you or forsake you! He'll be with you until the end. I learned this the hard way. Also, I have a new book coming out within the next year titled *"A Look in the Rearview Mirror,"* which I am co-authoring with my stage coordinator at Whosoever Outreach who is a close personal friend of mine; Mark Walker. This is a book about the hardships and miracles of starting a ministry. A collection of sermons from the beginning of my ministry plus much more! How to start a ministry from the ashes of your life! Be sure to look for it.

Stay updated at: www.NateFortnerMinistries.webs.com

Also view Nate's Author Bio page at:
www.WhosoeverPress.com

Be Doers of the Word

I just want to say how proud I am to call Nate my friend. Nate is always close by when I need him at the church. Nate's willingness to do even the most insignificant tasks, just to further the kingdom, is so appreciated. It is very exciting to see how God is working in his ministry. Nate is the epitome of a go-getter. He is driven by his passion to succeed in everything he sets his mind to. I think of James 1:22 in relation to how Nate carries himself. When he is inspired by God, to the best of his ability, he makes it happen. Congratulations Nate, on this great work. God bless. I love you like a brother.

Worship Pastor Chad Hallcox
Boaz Church Of God
www.Boazcog.com

About Nate Fortner Ministries

Whosoever Outreach

Whosoever is an Evangelistic Outreach ministry that was born after a conversation that I had with a Jehovah's Witness one day! He was basically telling me that I was a devil worshipper because only 144,000 people were going to heaven and I wasn't one of them. But what really kicked me in the face was the fact that he was a Jehovah's Witness and he said that he wasn't getting to go to heaven. At that moment, I immediately sent out a 911 prayer to God and asked Him to give me a way to reach this man. I realized that this man had put his faith in a dead hope! So I prayed again and asked God to give me a verse or a word. God give me something to reach this guy. Then it was like a machine gun going off in my soul W-H-O-S-O-E-V-E-R. I knew that the Bible said for whosoever would call upon the name of the Lord would be saved, and I took that as my answer from God. Thus resulting in Whosoever Outreach. I never intended on having a Thursday night Whosoever service. My plan was to go to drug rehab centers, jails, and churches preaching whosoever, because God also poured a sermon like no other into my spirit. I guess Whosoever on Thursday nights was God's idea! I once heard it said that if God didn't hurry up and judge America He'd have to apologize to Sodom and Gomorrah, but He spoke and said to me If He doesn't hurry up and judge the church, He's going to have to apologize to Sodom and Gomorrah! He spoke to me and said to stop judging and pushing people away just because their different! STOP looking at the drug addict as a drug addict! STOP looking at the drunk as a drunk! STOP looking at the Homosexual as a Homosexual! STOP pushing them away and start reaching out to them! There's room at the cross for them too! Start looking at them through Jesus' eyes; as a Whosoever! The church needs to stop condemning people to Hell before they even get there and start preaching forgiveness, healing, and deliverance again! When we start condemning others, we are denying the fact that we serve a God who is still in the saving business! The Cutters, homosexuals, drug addicts, religious cults, Adulterers, murderers, hurting people, anyone who doesn't have a relationship with Jesus Christ is a Whosoever! There's good news though! I don't care what you've done or where you been because Jesus still loves lost sinners! Yes! Sin is wrong, but it's not our job to judge, it's our job to show the love of Christ!

We meet every Thursday night at 1:30 A.M. for worship for second shift workers. Everyone is welcome. Our start time is actually Friday morning at 1:30 A.M. We perform dramas, have special speakers, Singer's, Programs, outreach in the community, and cook out's at

1:30 in the morning, etc…

Come join us in worship at The Flipside Youth Building at Boaz Church of God for Whosoever Outreach Service in beautiful Boaz, Alabama! Also visit us online at:

www.NateFortnerMinistries.webs.com

UPDATE: Do to circumstances beyond our control we are no longer able to hold the Thursday night 1:30 AM service. However, Nate Fortner is still available to come and minister at Churches of all sizes.

About the Author

I have always had a hard time finding the right words to say when I pray. There have been multiple times in my life that I would pray the best I knew how and ask God to teach me an out loud prayer. I didn't want to pray out loud to be seen, but I wanted to pray in a way that would be pleasing to God. The Holy Spirit then began to reveal to me through the Word of God Biblical principles that are fail proof on how to pray powerful and effective prayers that will reach the throne of God! Since then, I have received healing in my body, seen friends and family miraculously saved, and now I run a ministry that is reaching out to the world. I currently live in the small town of Boaz, Alabama where I'm in leadership in the Boaz Church of God under Pastor Ryan Bristow. I am also actively engaged in music ministry and I love to sing!

Resources

For a complete updated list of products we have available, please visit

www.WhosoeverPress.com

Our new online TV ministry "Whosoever Means Anybody" will be coming soon to:

www.NateFortnerMinistries.webs.com

www.Crosswalk.com

www.OutreachMagazine.com

http://buddysheets.tripod.com/hebrewwordsfor praise.htm

http://www.justworship.com/hebrewpraiseword s.php

http://www.agapebiblestudy.com

www.TimeToLetGo.com

Editorial Department

Did you find an error in this book? Let our editors know about it. Send us an e-mail to: Christy@ChristySmith.net. Let us know what page, paragraph, and sentence to check. If our editors feel that the wording needs changed, you will be rewarded. You will receive a FREE book or either a FREE CD signed by Nate Fortner for helping us clean up our act! LOL Thanks for your help and God Bless you and your family!

Write a review

So how did you like "TEACHING CHRISTIANS TO PRAY THE BIBLE WAY?" Well here's your chance to tell me about it. Go to www.Amazon.com. Type my name (Nate Fortner) in the search box. When a new screen appears, scroll down the page until you see the cover of "TEACHING CHRISTIANS TO PRAY THE BIBLE WAY." When you find it, click on the book. Then a page will appear just for this book. Then click on the button that says write a review and follow the simple instructions. Thanks so much and I hope you many awesome moments in prayer with our Lord and Savior Jesus Christ! It is my most heartfelt prayer for you that your prayer life is revolutionized!

149

150

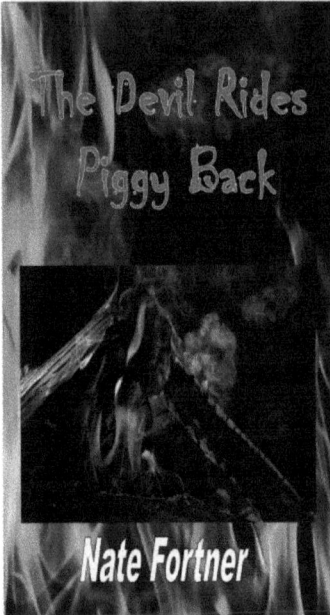

Brought To You By:

Whosoever
Press

152

Is Jesus the Lord of your life?
The Way To Jesus Christ
Is Simple:

1. ADMIT THAT YOU'RE A SINNER.
> For all have sinned, and come short of the glory of God.
> ROMANS 3:23

2. BELIEVE THAT JESUS IS GOD THE SON WHO PAID THE WAGES OF YOUR SIN.
> For the wages of sin is death (Eternal Separation from God): but the gift of God is eternal life through Jesus Christ our Lord.
> ROMANS 6:23

3. CALL UPON GOD.
> If thou shall confess with thy mouth the Lord Jesus and shall believe in your heart that God raised Him from the dead, You shall be saved!
> ROMANS 10:9

Repeat this prayer and mean it from your heart and you will be saved!

Dear Jesus, I'm a sinner. I'm sorry for my sin. I know You died on a cross for my sins to forgive me. Jesus, forgive me of my sins Lord. I believe that You died and rose again on the third day and now Your in heaven at the right hand of the Father praying for me! Take my sins away and remember them no more. Cast them Lord as far as the east is from the west! Jesus thank You for Your gift of grace! Make me a new creation. Cover me with Your blood and make me white as snow! Help me Lord to grow closer to You through Your Word and prayer. Amen!

www.ingramcontent.com/pod-product-compliance
Lightning Source LLC
Chambersburg PA
CBHW061722020426
42331CB00006B/1056